PLANT STEMS & ROOTS

David M. Schwartz is an award-winning author of children's books, on a wide variety of topics, loved by children around the world. *Dwight Kuhn's* scientific expertise and artful eye work together with the camera to capture the awesome wonder of the natural world.

For a free color catalog describing Gareth Stevens Publishing's list of high-quality books and multimedia programs, call 1-800-542-2595 (USA) or 1-800-461-9120 (Canada). Gareth Stevens Publishing's Fax: (414) 225-0377.

Library of Congress Cataloging-in-Publication Data

Schwartz, David M.
     Plant stems and roots / by David M. Schwartz; photographs by Dwight Kuhn.
          p. cm. — (Look once, look again)
     Includes bibliographical references and index.
     Summary: Highlights stems and roots, the essential plant parts that give us
radishes, blackberries, peas, milkweed, corn, strawberries, and trees.
     ISBN 0-8368-2581-0 (lib. bdg.)
     1. Stems (Botany)—Juvenile literature. 2. Roots (Botany)—Juvenile literature.
[1. Stems (Botany). 2. Roots (Botany). 3. Plants.] I. Kuhn, Dwight, ill. II. Title.
III. Series: Schwartz, David M. Look once, look again.
QK646.S42 2000
581.4'9—dc21   99-047692

This North American edition first published in 2000 by
Gareth Stevens Publishing
1555 North RiverCenter Drive, Suite 201
Milwaukee, Wisconsin 53212 USA

First published in the United States in 1998 by Creative Teaching Press, Inc., P. O. Box 6017, Cypress, California, 90630-0017.

Text © 1998 by David M. Schwartz; photographs © 1998 by Dwight Kuhn. Additional end matter © 2000 by Gareth Stevens, Inc.

Printed in the United States of America

1 2 3 4 5 6 7 8 9 04 03 02 01 00

1001242 Plant stems & roots

PLANT STEMS & ROOTS

by David M. Schwartz

photographs by Dwight Kuhn

A SPRINGBOARDS INTO SCIENCE SERIES

Gareth Stevens Publishing

MILWAUKEE

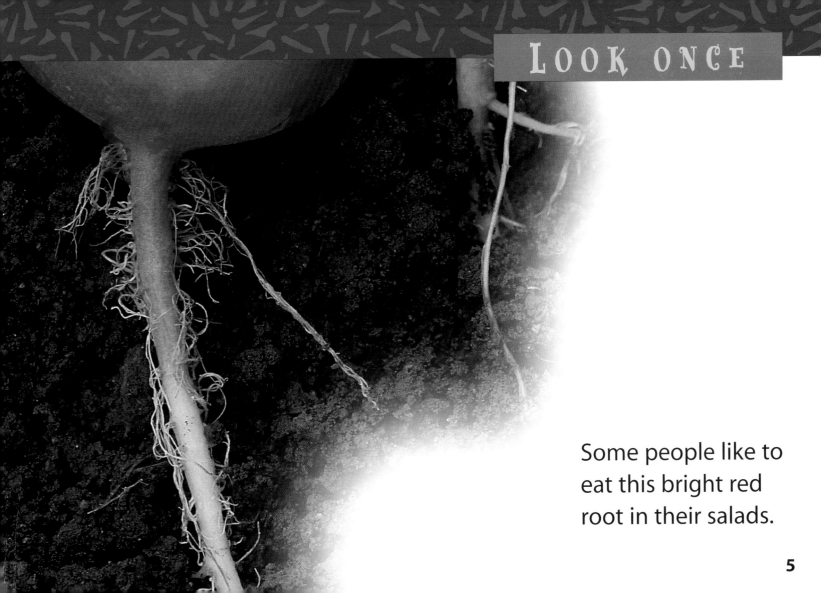

Some people like to eat this bright red root in their salads.

A radish has a root that swells up to store food for the plant. This kind of root is called a taproot. Hairs at the bottom of the root absorb water and minerals from the soil.

This is a view of a trunk. However, it is not the kind you pack with treasures!

7

The trunk of this oak tree, or any tree, is its stem. Every year, a tree grows a new ring of wood on its trunk. The age of a tree can be determined by counting its rings.

Try not to get too close to this thorny stem when you are picking berries.

Blackberry stems have delicious fruit. They also have sharp thorns. Animals would like to eat the young, green stems, but they don't like a mouthful of thorns!

These brown lumps are found on the roots of certain plants. This particular plant also bears tasty food in pods.

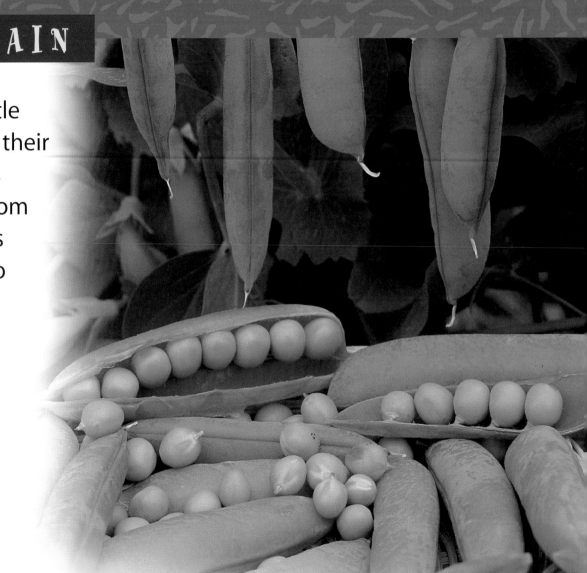

Pea plants have little brown nodules on their roots. The nodules absorb nitrogen from the soil. The plants use the nitrogen to make food.

Inside the stem of this plant
is a milky white sap.

13

Milkweed sap looks like milk, but it is not. Be careful; it is poisonous to people. Monarch butterfly caterpillars feed on milkweed sap. Birds avoid eating these caterpillars because the sap will make them sick.

This plant looks like it is walking on stilts.

15

The little "legs" of a corn plant are called prop roots. They help brace the corn against the wind.

Some plants make new plants from their stems. That's good for people who like this plant's sweet, red fruit.

17

Strawberry plants send out long, creeping stems called runners. Where the runners touch the ground, new strawberry plants take root. In this way, strawberry plants quickly spread.

A.

B.

C.

D.

E.

F.

G.

Look closely. Do you know to which plants these stems and roots belong?

A. Radishes

B. Oak tree

C. Blackberries

D. Peas

E. Milkweed

F. Corn

G. Strawberry

How many were you able to identify correctly?

fruit: the usually edible final product of certain plants.

minerals: simple chemicals or compounds found in the soil.

nitrogen: an element in the soil that is necessary for plants to grow.

nodules: small, knotlike outgrowths of plants.

pods: natural containers for fruit or seeds.

poisonous: toxic, deadly.

prop roots: structures that can grow above the ground to support the stem of a plant.

root: a normally underground portion of a plant that absorbs water and minerals for the plant.

runners: slender, creeping stems of a plant that lay down roots.

sap: a watery liquid that contains nourishment for plants.

stem: the main stalk of a plant that supports the plant.

stilts: poles or posts that lift a person or a structure off the ground.

swells: gradually grows in size, such as when air enters a balloon.

taproot: the main root of a plant that grows straight down.

thorns: sharp, pointed structures on a plant.

trunk: the woody stem of a tree.

ACTIVITIES

Greetings!

Make a greeting card out of a tree trunk rubbing. Carefully tape a piece of paper onto the trunk of a tree. Rub the side of a crayon over the paper until the pattern of the tree trunk appears. Fold the paper in half twice, and you've made your own nature greeting card.

Carrot Top

The carrot is a root vegetable with long, lacy leaves. The part you eat grows under the ground, and the green leaves grow above the ground. The next time you eat a carrot, save the green end of it that still has the leaves intact. (This won't work with the popular mini-carrot variety found in the grocery store.) Place the end of the carrot in a saucer that contains water. Add water as necessary, and a new carrot will eventually grow.

Lemon Seed, Very Pretty

Each time you eat fresh fruit or vegetables, such as an apple, a pear, a pea, a bean, or a lemon, save some of the seeds. Put the seeds in separate containers of soil. Keep the containers in a sunny location, and water them a little every day. Observe the containers from time to time to see what might be growing.

Compost

Compost is organic matter used for fertilizing the soil. The first step in creating compost is to save kitchen scraps, such as vegetables, fruit, egg shells, and coffee grounds. Do not save meat or bones. To hold the scraps, build a compost bin with some fencing. If you'd prefer something fancier, there are many different designs for do-it-yourself compost bins on the Internet and at the library.

More Books to Read

Bloodthirsty Plants. Victor Gentle (Gareth Stevens)
Coping with Food Trash. Trash Busters (series). Jamie Daniel and Veronica Bonar (Gareth Stevens)
Exploring the Science of Nature (series). Jane Burton and Kim Taylor (Gareth Stevens)
Flowers, Trees, and Fruits. Sally Morgan (Kingfisher)
Natural Food and Products. Gary Chandler (Twenty-first Century Library)
Potato. Barrie Watts (Silver Burdett)
Trees, Leaves, and Bark. Young Naturalist Field Guides (series). Diane L. Burns (Gareth Stevens)

Videos

Food for the City: Produce. (Phoenix/BFA)
Look What I Grew: Windowsill Gardens. (Library Video)
Magical Farm and Foods. (Lyrick Studios)

Web Sites

www.vg.com/cgi-bin/v2/gemag/s=4569
www.familyeducation.com/article/0,1120,1-571,00.html

Some web sites stay current longer than others. For further web sites, use your search engines to locate the following topics: *berries, fruits, gardening, roots, stems, trees,* and *vegetables.*

INDEX

animals 10, 14

berries 9, 10, 18, 19, 20
birds 14

caterpillars 14
corn 15, 16, 19, 20

fruit 9, 10, 17, 18, 19, 20

hairs 6

milkweed 13, 14, 19, 20
minerals 6
monarch butterfly caterpillars 14

nitrogen 12
nodules 11, 12, 19

oak trees 8, 20

peas 11, 12, 19, 20

pods 11, 12
poisonous sap 14
prop roots 16, 19

radishes 5, 6, 19, 20
rings, tree 7, 8
roots 5, 6, 11, 12, 16, 18, 19
runners 18, 19

sap 13, 14, 19
soil 6, 12
stems 7, 8, 9, 10, 13, 17, 18, 19
stilts 15

taproots 6, 19
thorns 9, 10, 19
tree rings 7, 8, 19
trees 7, 8, 19, 20
trunks, tree 7, 8, 19